Motherhood in Verse: Quiet Thoughts of a Tired Mom

Eryn Richard

BookLeaf Publishing

India | USA | UK

Presentation by *BookLeaf Publishing*

Web: www.bookleafpub.com

E-mail: info@bookleafpub.com

ISBN: 9789358367850

First edition 2023

For the little ones who call me Mommy. You're the reason for everything I do.

Reading is Everything

First night home, the pull of sleep pushing to
dreams.
Daddy's voice, a low hypnotizing hum,
"Goodnight moon..."
The first of many adventures that will teach you
everything.

Two and fast. Always moving. Always
chattering.
Exploring new worlds. Learning. Laughing.
Living through words.
Tucked in tight with a goodnight kiss,
"I love you right up to the moon - and back."

Kindergarten with big dreams. New friends.
School rules!
Circle time adventures with Mrs. Tucker.
And the morning message: "Be bright so no
shadows can stay."

Third grade curiosity with reading gains in leaps
and bounds.
After school clubs and pizza prizes.
Healthy competition creating forever friends.

"How do you spell love? You don't spell it, you feel it."

Twelve years old and sixth grade proud.
Class-leader and adventure seeker...of the literary variety.
Easy friend and "kinder than is necessary."

Fifteen, sunbeam on the window seat. Crisp cover, creased for the first time. The next adventure awaits.
Leaning on words to navigate (high school is hard).
"Stay gold, Ponyboy. Stay gold."

Eighteen and college-bound.
Crossing the stage to the mic with a message for your friends:
"Live! Live the wonderful life that is in you!"

Four years pass in a flash. Reading education summa cum laude.
Already hired. Motivated. Elevated.
"Today is your day. Your mountain is waiting."
New wife, first home, big plans, endless dreams.

First night home, the pull of sleep pushing to dreams.

Your voice, a low hypnotizing hum, "Goodnight
moon..."
The first of many adventures that will teach her
everything.

References
Stanzas 1/9 - Goodnight Moon by Margaret
Wise Brown (1947)
Stanza 2 - Guess How Much I Love You by Sam
McBratney (1994)
Stanza 3 - The Wonderful Things You Will Be
by Emily Winfield Martin (2015)
Stanza 4 - Winnie the Pooh by A. A. Milne
(1926)
Stanza 5 - Wonder by R. J. Palacio (2012)
Stanza 6 - The Outsiders by S.E. Hinton (1967)
Stanza 7 - The Picture of Dorian Gray by Oscar
Wilde (1890)
Stanza 8 - Oh the Places You'll Go by Dr. Seuss
(1990)

Ode to Spring Breaking the Clutches of the Cold

Come December, winter's cold has seeped into
my veins,
Wrapped it's icy fingers around my heart and
Pulled a hood of doubt over my eyes.
Fearing the bitterness of winter permanent,
Spring appears.
First with the unjust tease of warmer days,
Like a broken promise, air returns to ice.
Then longer stays melt the frost to dew–
Lifting the lingering hours of winter doom,
Thawing the blue from my bones.
On morning walks, spring sounds awaken as the
earth comes alive.
Whistle. Chirp. Warble. Flutters of wings
making nests in trees.
Cherry buds open, the warming breezes bring
notes of vanilla, almond, rose.
I look up.
The sun's warmth coaxing some color and
freckles from pale cheeks.
Shedding winter's weight, I embrace Spring!
Thank you for wrapping your arms around my
cold and frantic heart.

For raising morale. For bringing hope. For
promising that easier days draw near.
Thank you SPRING for bursts of color
Cutting through the brown and gray. For
motivation and new life.
Now with the rejuvenating early light and later
evenings,
I can accomplish anything!

To Tired Moms Everywhere

To new moms, anxious and scared, who
constantly doubt,
Who go unsupported to figure it out,
With books, and blogs, and frequent doc calls,
With your best laid plans dissipating,
Whose every minute, hour, and day is to care,
And despite unsolicited advice,
You know all things instinctively.

To veteran moms, outnumbered and
overwhelmed,
Who go date-night-less and unfulfilled,
With negative time for clutter and laundry,
With long days and short years stealing your
shine,
Whose every motion, decision, and expression is
for them,
And with disadvantaged means,
You make everyone balanced and fair.

To other moms, tired and broken, who struggle
with the weight of the mental load,
Who go unseen, unheard, invalidated, ignored,
With the re-done messy bun, and the uneaten
meals prepared with love,
With your early grays and dark-circled eyes
stealing your age,

Whose every thought, breath, beat, and step is to
serve,
And with cards stacked against the impossible
bar,
You perfect the unnoticed deeds.

To all moms everywhere, I see you.
You are strong with resilience like a spring
And those little things–the details, the seams–
Like a well-oiled machine even on days when
you're struggling.
You are the underpinning, the footing and
bedrock,
Breaking the chains that raised you.
Your children are the light in this newly dark
world,
And like you, they are indestructible.
Taking the tools taught and passing them on–
Your stability and warmth imbues the very fabric
of their being.
It's extraordinary, the work that you do,
Never forget, you've done it so well.
In the end, all your mistakes fall away, forgotten.
Remembered only are the laughs, and stories
and songs,
Birthday dinners, good advice, a shoulder to cry
on, and
Arms open wide.

I am not creative

I am not a poet watching the blink blink blink
of cursor on blank screen, searching for locution
and afflatus anew, working past the night
when the first cool drops of light creep through
cracks–
warming the living room.

I am not a writer pressing pen to page, fumbling
with words
creating conflict, character, climax, and in
cathartic release
like the peregrine–with newly healed
wings–released,
a story appears, then forgotten between
notebook pages
gathering dust.

I am not an artist cloaked in pastel, struggling in
shadow and light
to bring underpainting to life and layering the
cerulean, ultramarine
and beryl waves with foam verisimilar in a
clichéd beach scene.

I am not a singer perfectly tuned, breathing
melody
in belts and trills and perfect shower acoustics
with once-recorded voice from years ago–
talent wasted by a different life of duty and
priorities
now sings baby-named lullabies.

But I am a mother whose heart grew five times
over and
at rest and in beat sits with two open wounds for
the babies
never held, who tirelessly (and sometimes
tiredly) teaches to read and count,
to share, that feelings are valid, to love your
body,
and above all else: KINDNESS.
A mother who cooks and cleans and plans and
RSVPs and sometimes shouts
and unapologetically neglects–but only herself.

Saturday Morning Ballet

Saturday mornings with my oldest, the
born-to-be big sister,
frustratingly begin with a fight–"I hate ballet!"
And yet,
her prancing step, grace, and inclination for
performance say otherwise.
Breakfast is key, but like the honey badger not to
be preyed,
she defends her hungerless state with fury and
ire.
Every week, repeat…what am I doing wrong?
I was the same (so my dad says), but this
karmic routine is older than old and tiring.

And then finally after a few bites–sometimes at
the table,
sometimes in the car–the clouds clear and the
storminess fades.
Fire replaced by sparkle, her eyes light up.
Angry eyebrows dissipate,
charismatic giggle returned.
Oh my heart!
My sweet girl,
affectionate and amenable except when she's
not.

On the way, with little sister in tow, the stories
and questions ensue…
"Yesterday at school…"
"Mommy look…"
"Did you know…?"
"Mommy how did…?"
"Mommy why do…?"
I turn the music up click by click,
creating space between my thoughts and her
words.
My annoyance doesn't abate so easily.

Then at the studio: Determined. Inspired. Fluent.
I am in awe of the girl she is growing to be.
I watch for a minute,
before sneaking to the lobby for convo and ice
tea
and with baby in tow. But not really a baby any
more.
Here in the lobby with familiarity and a friend,
I'm in awe again.
How did my girls, once so small and dependent
and completely fixated on me, become the
running, laughing, dancing, jumping, talking,
leading,
caring, climbing, learning, sharing, protecting,
free-spirited ones with me today?

Where it Wasn't

It was on the breakfast bar,
exactly where I left it.
Except it wasn't.
Overwhelmed a few nights before
by the tidiness. Clean surfaces.
Carpet fresh lingering in the air.
Bottles washed and drying.
Dogs fed. Walked.
Vacuum still warm,
and cord UNwrapped on the floor,
(but I barely noticed).
How did he do it all with three needy, active
kids,
shadowing his every gesture, questioning every
move,
and still manage outdoor play and minimal
screens?
Amidst the gratitude - what was it?
Maybe shame.

Then tonight, dawned by the urgency of her
birthday,
two days away.
No it was today, but there was a party to prepare.
"Did you see the gold glitter spray?"

It was on the breakfast bar.
"Never saw it."
But it was on the breakfast bar.
Where I left it.
Irritation clear in his tired, furrowed brow.
His gravelly tone - maybe annoyance.
(Probably annoyance.)
But it was on the breakfast bar.

So I cleaned again.
But not in ways I normally do:
I emptied the trash onto the floor,
squinting for a flicker of gold.
Was it in the box? No once more.
I checked again, the breakfast bar,
where I left it, and over again it wasn't there.

Suddenly spent, I accepted defeat.
For all the places it wasn't and should've been.
And ascended the steps heavily.
Irritation clear on my tired, furrowed brow.
My gravelly tone - definitely annoyance.
"I left it on the breakfast bar."

a haiku for mornings with my children

school days' lethargy-
frequent wakes and running late.
weekends, sleep in? no.

Hard Times Are Best

A longing for consistent nighttime sleep,
like an impoverished hunger…relentless.
Multiple wakings to cries or wet beds or
intrusive thoughts or
overheard midnight candy raids and TV.
Drawing rest from anxiety-fueled dreams,
and each morning, waking to the RING RING
RING.
Too early.

These days are hard, unbalanced
and with guilt like the desert sun…relentless.
Wake, work, reset, sleep– on repeat,
each day longer than before and then they're
gone.
And weekends, faster still, with lack of structure
and time, desperately looking for the pause
button…
Just one more day at home before
the dread seeps in.
Please.

One day I'll miss these days–the days of small–
and be longing for those sleepless nights again

where I rock and snuggle and sing into early
morning shine.
These nights when the "Mamas" shatter my
dreams and
two little hands and pink cheeks peek over the
railing.
These nights when the "I had a bad dream" slips
under the wrinkles of blanket and cuddles close
in an already-crowded bed.
And these nights when the quiet, self-sufficiency
of him scales cabinets and gates to find the
remote at 2AM.

By the time I miss these days, I will have
forgotten the mess.
So I hold these three little beating hearts to
mine–
(and the big heart too!)
and take pictures and trips and run errands and
dance and sing and cook and soak up the sun.
Because someday, "I wanna come!" becomes
"Do I have to?"
And it will be too late.

7th Period

The afternoon slump creeps in suddenly. Like a
heavy blanket,
cloaks my productivity,
pulls my eyelids
down
down
down.
Chin droops.
Breath deepens–was that a hint of a snore?
Muzzy voices fade as its irresistible song
weaves its fingers through my hair.
A third cup of coffee missed its mark
completely.
(And when they're out it's even worse.)
Sometimes a snack brings me back,
but they're usually gone.
Then I'm gone.
"Snap out of it!"
Staring at the screen, my senses replace the
dream
trying to take hold.
Fifteen minutes to go, new energy finishes one
more
impossible task before the bell. And with
another day behind me, I head home.

Late Night Poetry

How'd it get to be 1AM on the day of the dread?
Last time I checked, we'd just tucked them in.
This weekend was especially hard
with ceaseless rain, too-long-screens, and ER
threats.
So I took a few minute-turned hours to think and
create.
Tomorrow will surely bring the consequences of
squeezing
fifteen more minutes out of the night, even as
the day slips in.
And fifteen more.
And maybe fifteen more.
Yet still, I sit here, characters spring from my
typing hands
to fall into words and verse (but rarely rhyme)
on my screen.
Deadlines insist I push the limits of sleep.
The littlest little cries again–that makes four
times–
and I hear, "At least I'm still up."
As the muse leaves, I force out this one last line
and
task by task I check off the remaining million
things on my list.

Maybe

Maybe I can make the cut,
or meet the deadline,
or balance the budget in favor of black.
Maybe I can remember to remind in a
non-nagging way
or pause before I react.
Maybe I'll know when it's time for Baxter to die
or what to invest or where to eat.
Maybe one day I'll get enough sleep.
Is it even possible to swim in the maybe sea?
Or at least to float? Or tread water?
Maybe, we shall see.

Family First

Feeling the work-life balance scale tipping in the
wrong direction,
I took a day.
We boarded a bus, sunny overhead,
Rain barely spitting.
My daughter - deranged with excitement -
laughing, bouncing, asking
too many questions and I didn't have the
answers.
I put earbuds in, work-guilt still drifting through.
Something about the hum from the engine and
the music-drowned voices and
passing the massive houses in Chevy Chase -
gaudy and ornate.
At the zoo, the clouds break. A perfect day!
Music and coveted homes and work forgotten,
she grasps my hand.
We break off in separate groups -
a race to find each kid's project animal:
red panda, hedgehog, lion, bald eagle.
Not really a race, but certainly not enough time.
And the mile-long path (uphill both ways) with
more animals than those.
My daughter's red panda is first.

After a hunger-induced refusal and stomp and much coaxing,
she reads her notes, then it's on to the next!
The rest of the day a blur…
Bison, elephant!, cozy lunch spot (away from the bisons!),
giant panda, too many birds, tiger, lion, Przewalski's horse,
otter, turtle, barred owl, beaver, lemur, ferret, bobcat, sea lion, cheetah,
boarding the bus home, and plans to bring all my littles this summer.
Today was the stuff that personal days are made of.
The need fulfilled. And not enough pictures to capture it.

Work Week Mornings

22

Piercing alarm shatters oh-so-sweet dreams.
Didn't I just fall asleep? Snooze once.
The dreams come back easily,
Pulling me through the next nine minutes.
The alarm sounds again, jolting me from the
deep.
Snooze twice.
Nothing this time. Nine. Minutes. Fast.
Blaring, grating, alarming. Irritating. Snooze
once more.
Then the alarm sounds again to rally
"Maximum effort" for the day–just like any
other day.

The Little Things

All the things I miss…
folding warm laundry, fresh from the dryer,
completing a thought,
quiet stillness,
uninterrupted showers,
preparing meals that get eaten,
a worry-free empty house,
date nights,
accumulating sick leave,
sleeping in,
not sharing a meal,
spontaneity,
uncomplicated schedules,
quickly leaving the house,
saving money,
cooking for two,
a one-bedroom is enough,
fiscal fasts,
getting all the laundry done,
sleeping through the night,
working late without guilt,
friend dates,
weekend trips,
uncensored music and TV,
an organized desk,

knowing where my xyz is,
…are the things I would go a lifetime without
for them.

Guilty Summer

Summer is coming!
The taste of freedom almost on my tongue,
each day crawls forward, but the weekends still
pass too fast.
I need it. The summer.
Not ready and ready last September
at the same time.
Summer brings catching up,
lying back, and plans that will only half occur.
But it's okay because next year will be easier
and easier still the next.
Summer means pool days and storytime,
bike trail walks and lunchtime with Daddy.
Where the well-used patio glows greener
for maybe one more year, but probably two.
In summer things are just EASIER–
without the daily rush and impossible workload
and
deadlines, and lunches,
and late nights for all the wrong reasons.
Even so, I'll guiltily take my littlest littles to
school,
and with his tears and my broken heart,
I'll give the empty reminder of water play days.
By mid-July each tomorrow is like today.

I'll look for new adventures, and
some of them we'll do–
desperately trying to stave off August's dread.
But now, I long for summer.
And for six more creeping weeks,
I'll routinely live amidst enthusiasm and
anticipation
for what summer will bring.

About Him

I want to write a poem about him.
But finding the accurate words to say
what is in my heart and in my head is like
leaping from the tallest building, expecting to
fly.
He has always been here, even before he was,
somehow my heart knew to heal and grow and
wait.
A forgotten childhood fondness became
an instant connection. Again.
He is realistic and steady
to my impractical flight.
Together we have grown deep roots,
seeded by only ourselves,
and bloomed three bubbly flowers
who are the perfect mix of relentlessly strong
and exceptionally kind.
Even when it wasn't so shiny–
in leaving, he saved me, all those years before.
Only without him did I learn to pull myself out
of the bottomless trench.
But then he came back to brighten the dark
spaces in my heart
where he never really left.
And today, in humor and upset,

in health and fears,
in give up and fight harder, he always
plans one step ahead.
He knows more than I think,
and fills in the gaps,
compliments me so well,
listens and learns, and sternly but gently
tries to teach the hardest lessons in a different
way than he knew.
A father and partner in the deepest, truest sense.
Sometimes irked (as it goes), but mostly
grateful.
Always loved.

Why Am I Up So Late?

Under the guise of preparing for National Board,
I write this poem (and three before) to meet one
of many
overlapping deadlines that seem impossible -
and yet somehow I'll meet - and so
I borrow hours from sleep even though the
morning will be
terrible.
After submitting Component 3, inspiration
rushed around me,
I let my fingers lead and the words fell into
maybe clever lines on the screen.
The ripe excitement that comes with being
"almost done"
keeps my eyes open and thoughts focused and
alert.
Even after nearing 2am, I climb the stairs
and settle next to rhythmic snores, I continue to
write.
Just one more.
Reflecting on this challenge, I have a style
where
the flowery words I long for sometimes seem
fake and forced.

So I write simply about me, and things that
matter,
and things I feel.
And one by one the pieces settle into their
interlocking grooves,
revealing an intricate puzzle of all the things that
made me me.
A self portrait in words.
Now at 2:06, I really must get some sleep or be
completely
useless
to finish tomorrow.

90-Day Notice

Past 90 days and no letter–
Gasp!
Whatever surfaced this unknown is cruel and
dark…
after the sacrifice and commitments from the
year,
and the emptied bank account.
Realizing that we might be forced to make the
decision
we should've already made, I cleaned.
One space after another arranged, ordered.
Clear spaces bring clearer thoughts.
Tightness fades, racing thoughts quiet.
Tears brimming at the corner of my eyes, dry.
Music drowning out the noise. Grounded, I find
myself–
hopeful? Probably not, but close.
The day is spent in coded discussion,
with too many what-ifs and so the panic creeps
back in.
Busying myself with more, I somehow manage.
Senses return in remembering to let go of the
uncontrollable.
We will figure it out.
Everything will be okay.

Writer's Block

Can I write three more poems?
The words, dammed in my brain,
filter out letter by letter by letter.
They don't have to be good,
there is enough of good to just finish.
This is probably not the foot in the door, but
what fun and stressful it has been!
To say "I'm published," a dream. Ideally,
the kind of dream that wedges the foot in a door.
Just the toe, pushing until it swings–
but not so hard it slams shut again.
Could it really matter in this five-year plan?
Unplanned and unprepared, the minutes past
bedtime
tick, tick, tick, tick, tick.
Snacks on the way, I settle to pound the keys
once more,
ideas bottlenecked–just beyond what makes
sense.
Forced out now, a race to the end.
Now, can I just write two more?

Like Mother Like Daughter

I'm trying not to write my last two poems
about writing poems.
So I'll write about bedtime.
My first born daughter is me–
passive aggressive notes,
ignoring directions, creativity in dance,
and art, and song, a steadfast friend to a fault,
flighty and smart, all unchecked and confusing
feelings.
Trying to remember another way than what I
knew,
remaining calm, I tuck her in, ducking swings
and kicks, and just remind her that I love her.
But not quite like that.
After nearing an hour of intermittent tears mixed
with notes strapped to Sloth and hurled down the
stairs,
she sheepishly approaches: "I'm sorry."
Me too because I still haven't found another way
than I knew.
Restorative interaction looks like a normal
bedtime,
but this was the third night abruptly closing with
the end of song:
begging and tears.

In 14-20 years, if she is still me (something forbid!,
I'll know what to do, and maybe even before.
Broken and scared, I lived, navigated, and overcame it.
And she can too, even better than me.

On to the Next!

To finish what you start, is a challenge in itself.
But to complete it artfully, painfully,
neglectfully,
worriedly that it wasn't really worth the pain and
neglect,
this is a first!
The first follow-through–not backing
down–despite
voices whispering and shouting, "get out while
you still can!"
Unbounded limits prioritized the important and
major
tasks that pile endlessly on my desk, slumping
my shoulders, and wail
from sticky notes lining my walls.
And one more note removed, crumpled, thrown
away.
Not the expected relief, but an accomplishment
still.
Guilt remains that I've squandered hours and
days
meant for more necessary things.
Tonight I'll end when there's still some time for
sleep,
not enough, but more than before.

Pride will propel me through to the next
deadline,
precariously balancing what remains.